T0197050

Coloring Fun With Words

learn to spell and remember difficult words
through coloring.

Tracey H. Steffek

authorHOUSE®

AuthorHouse™
1663 Liberty Drive
Bloomington, IN 47403
www.authorhouse.com
Phone: 1-800-839-8640

Published by AuthorHouse   08/06/2012

ISBN: 978-1-4772-0633-1 (sc)
ISBN: 978-1-4772-0632-4 (e)

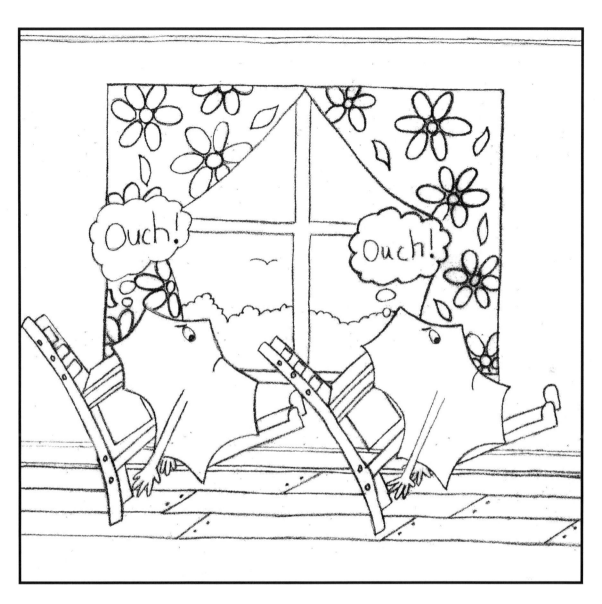

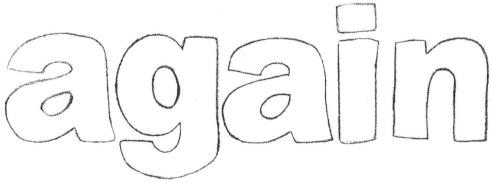

I fell out of my chair *again*.

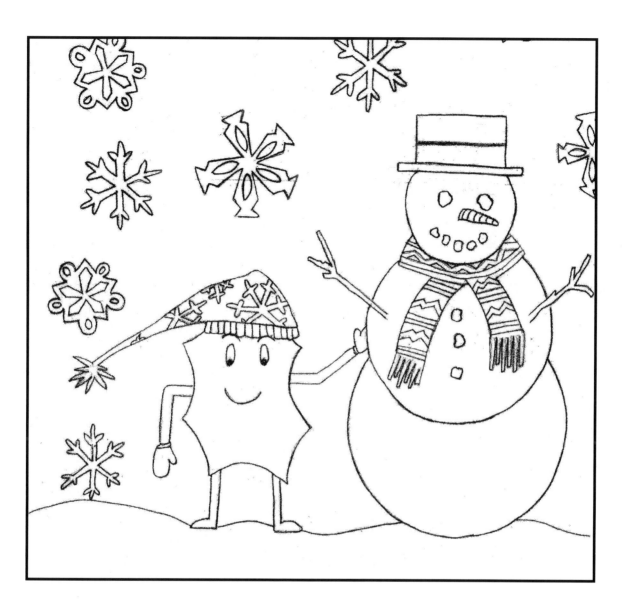

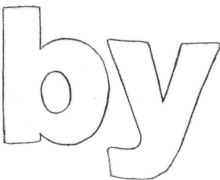

I am standing **by** the snowman.

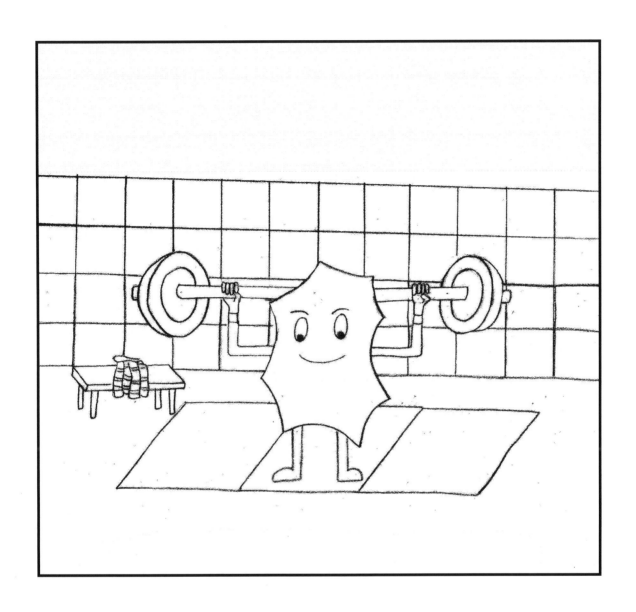

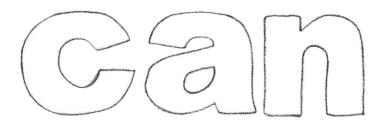

I *can* lift weights.

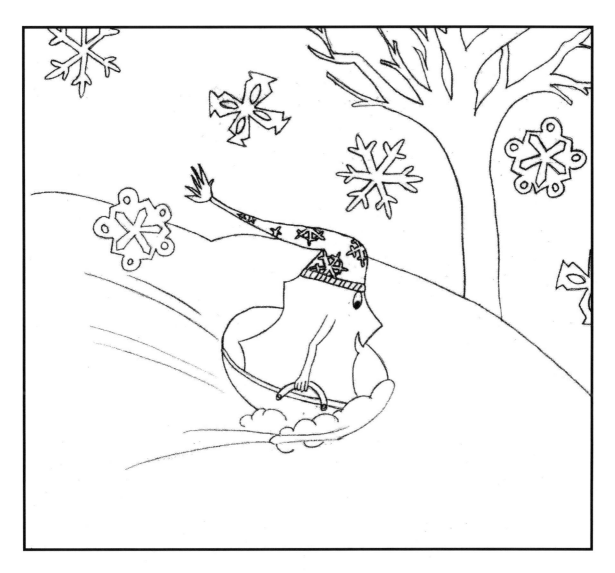

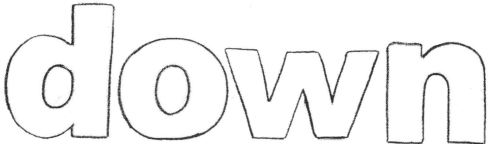

I like sliding **down** the hill on my saucer.

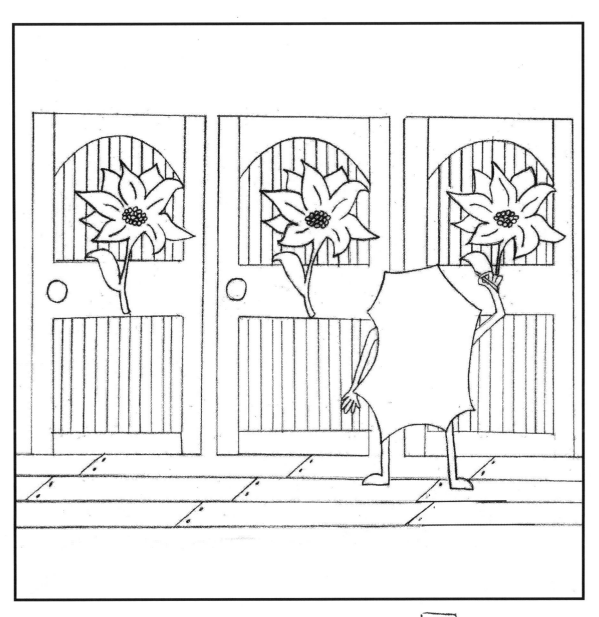

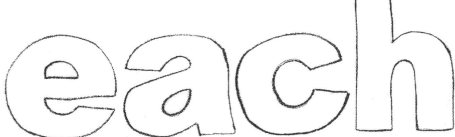

I drew a flower on *each* door.

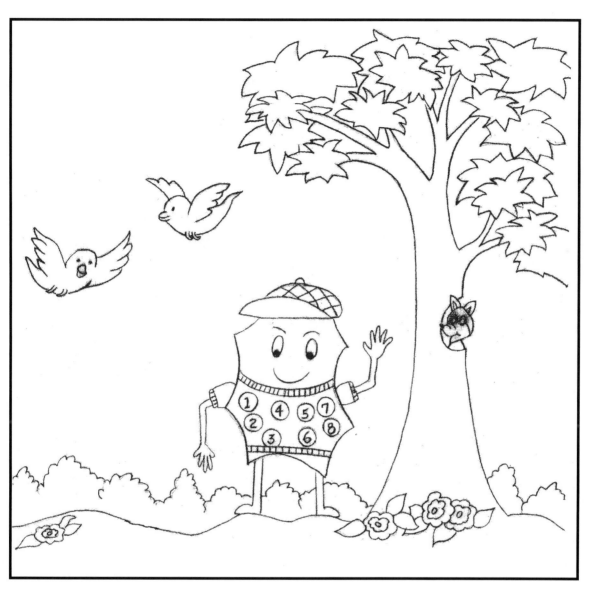

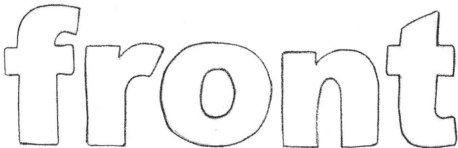

I have eight circles on the **_front_** of my shirt.

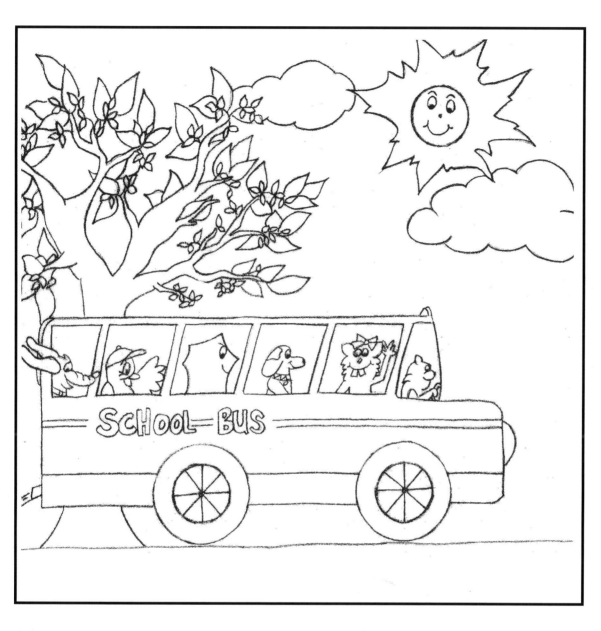

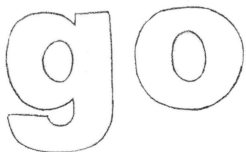

I *go* to school on the school bus.

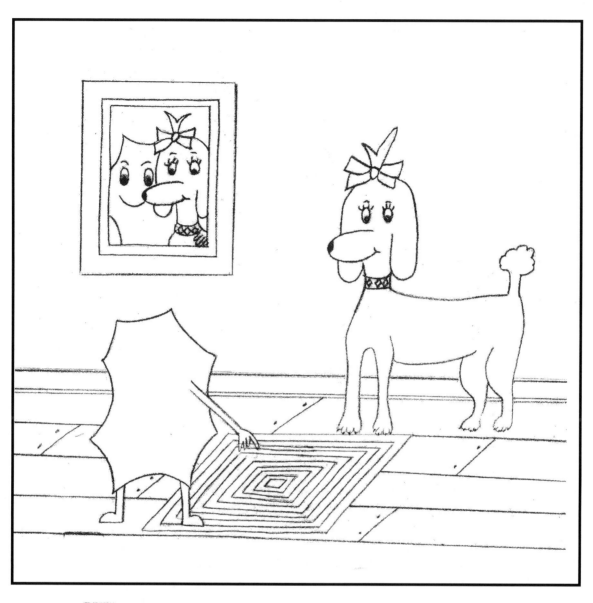

here

I tell my dog to "*come **here***".

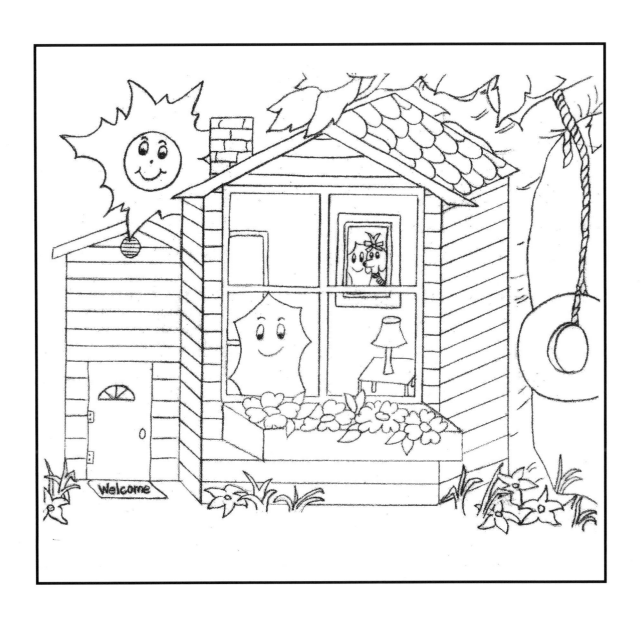

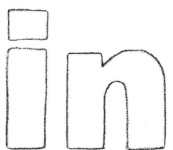

I am *in* my house.

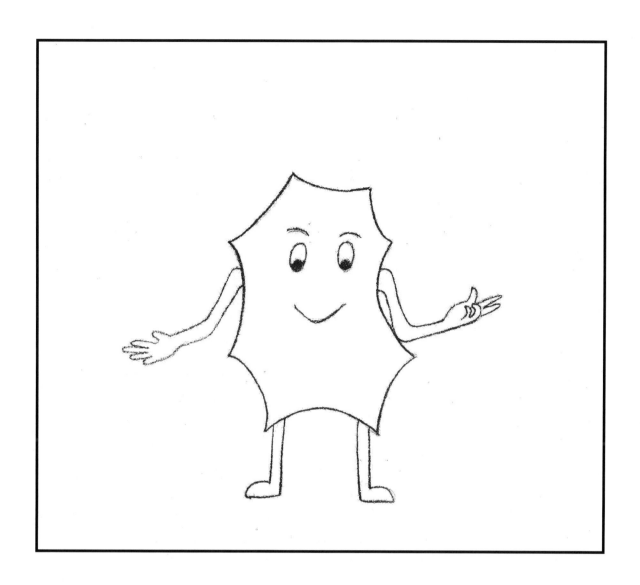

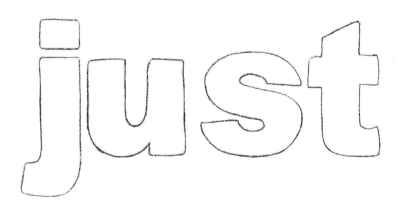

It's *just* me, nobody else.

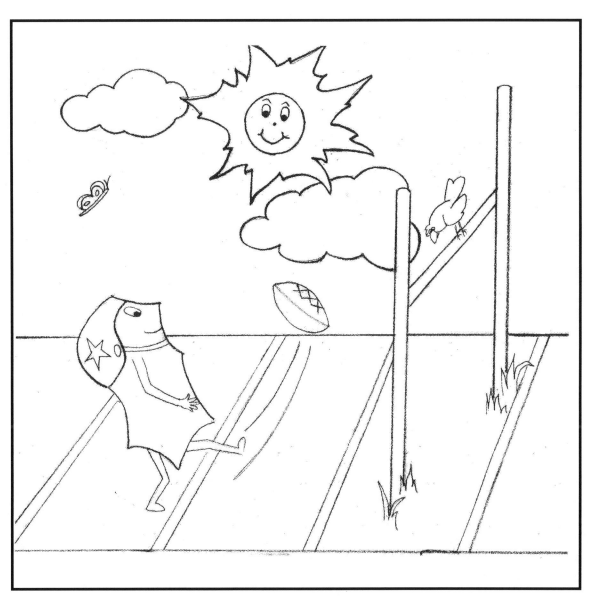

kick

I can ***kick*** the football.

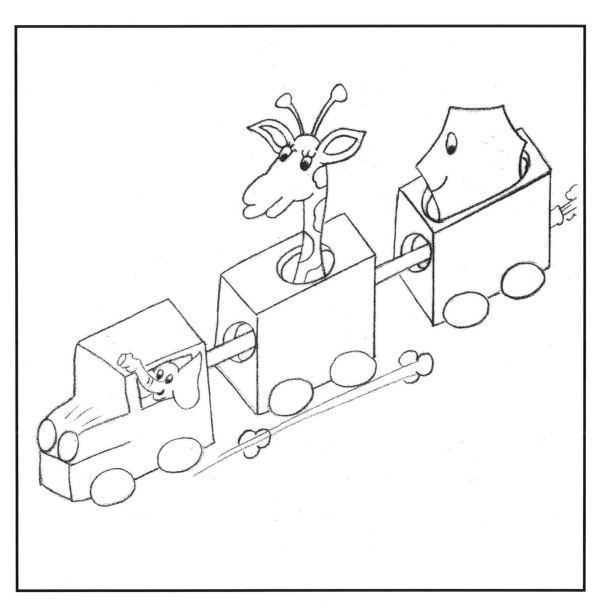

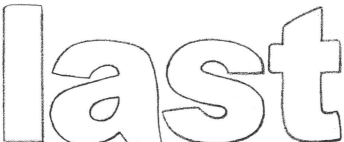

I'm in the **last** train car.

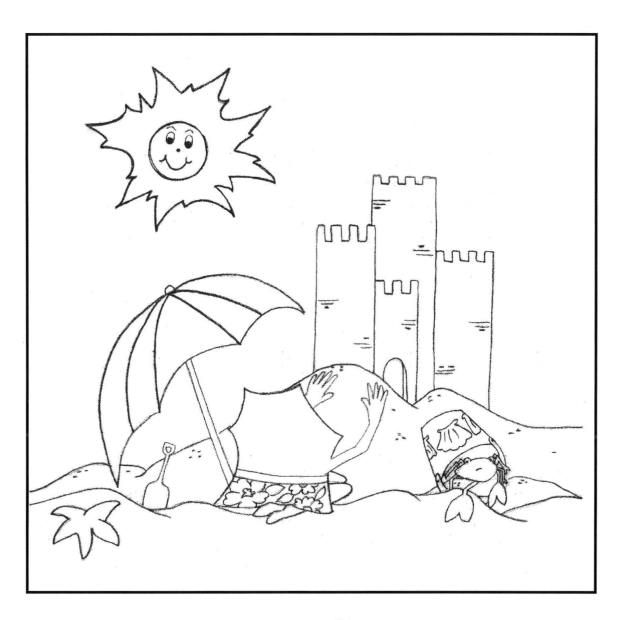

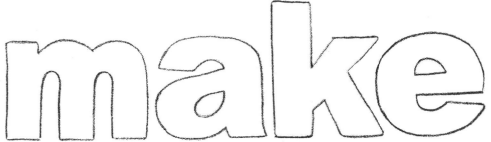

I can **make** a sand castle at the beach.

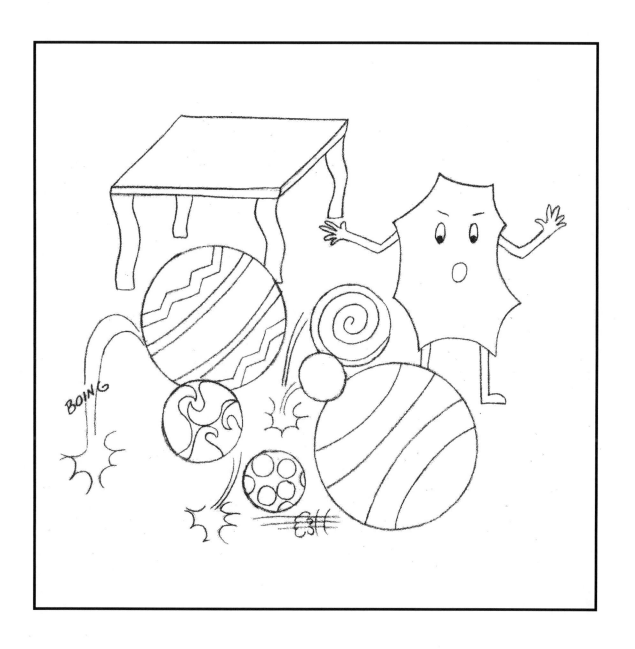

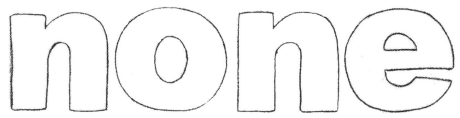

None of the balls are on the table.

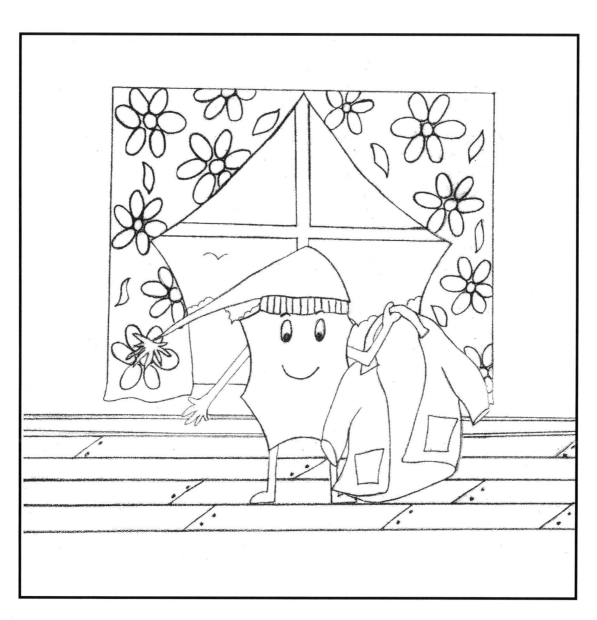

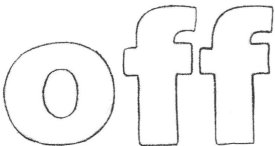

I took my jacket *off*.

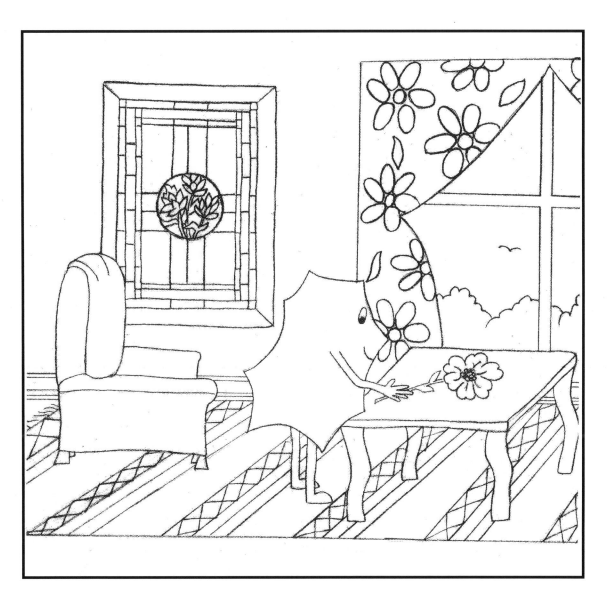

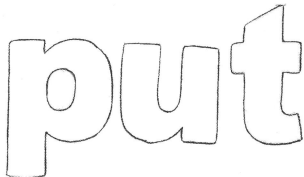

I ***put*** the flower on the table.

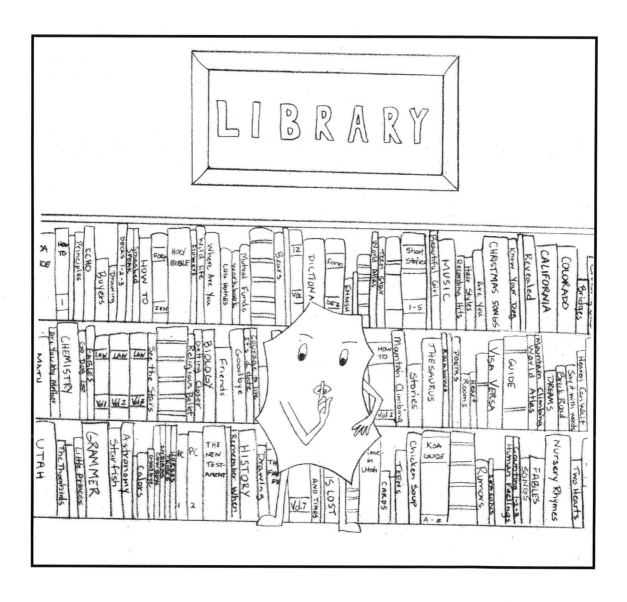

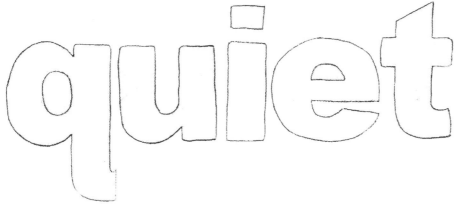

Please be *quiet* in the library.

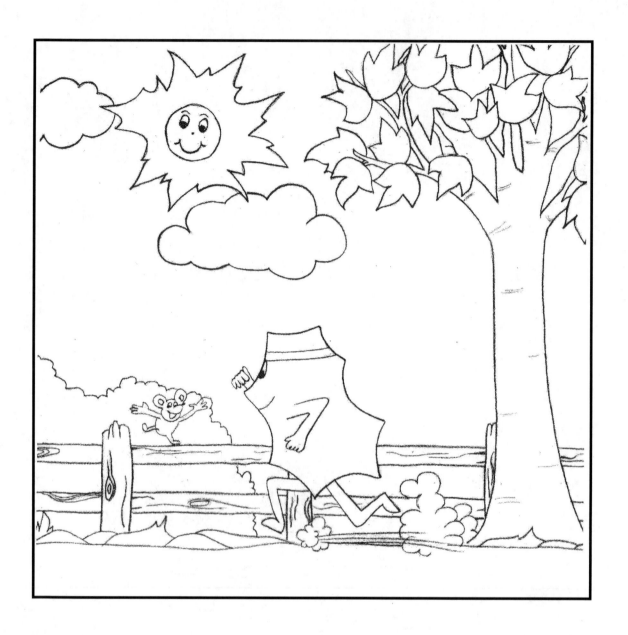

run

I like to *run*.

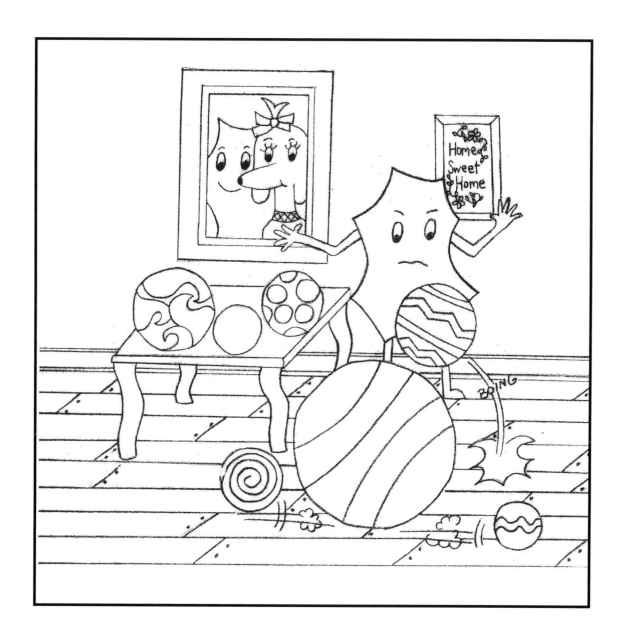

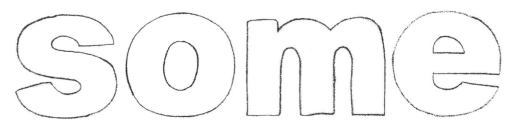

Some of the balls are on the table.

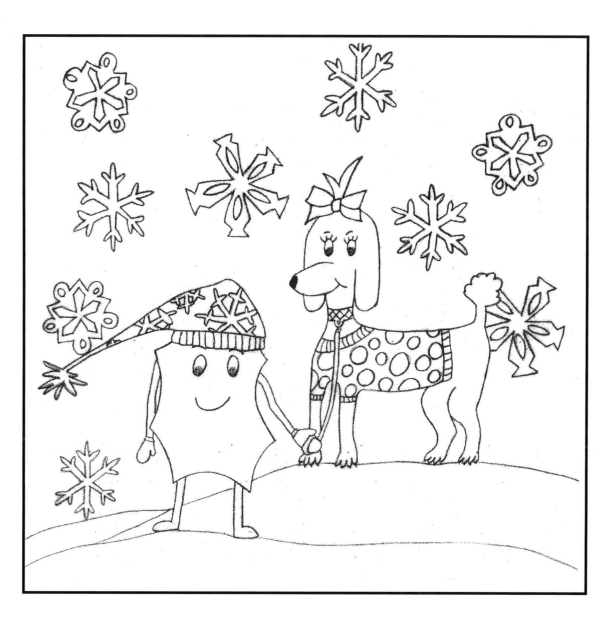

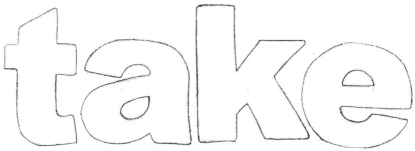

I *take* my dog for a walk everyday.

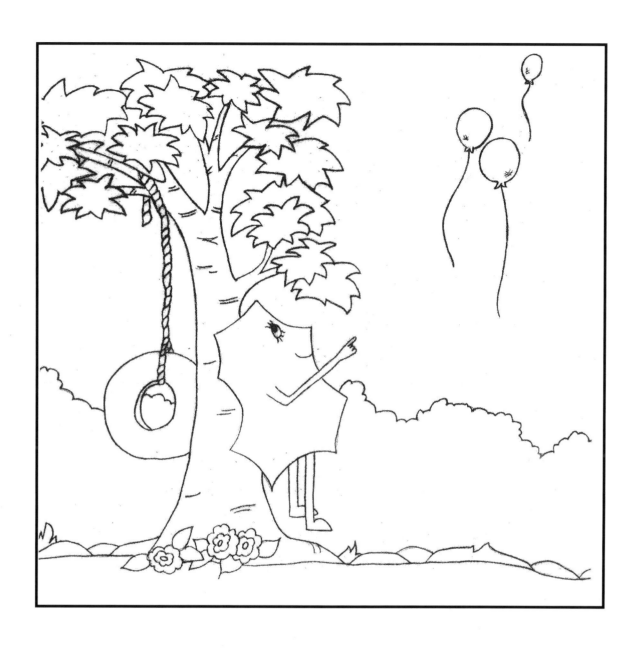

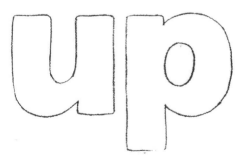

I am watching the balloons go **up**.

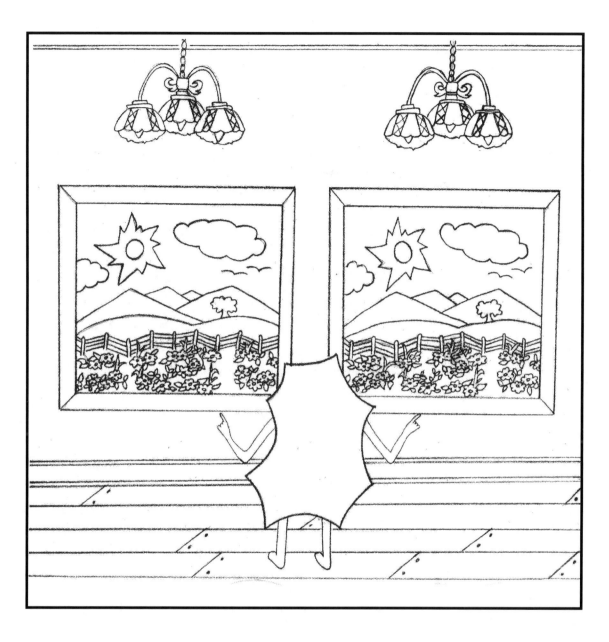

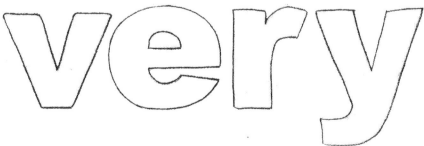

These pictures are the **very** same.

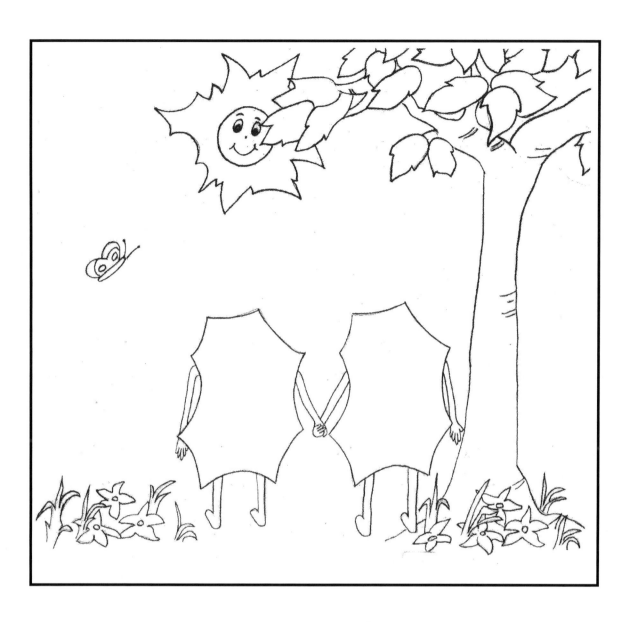

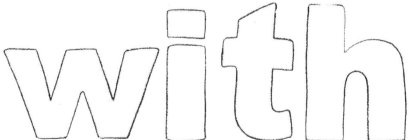

I like walking **with** you.

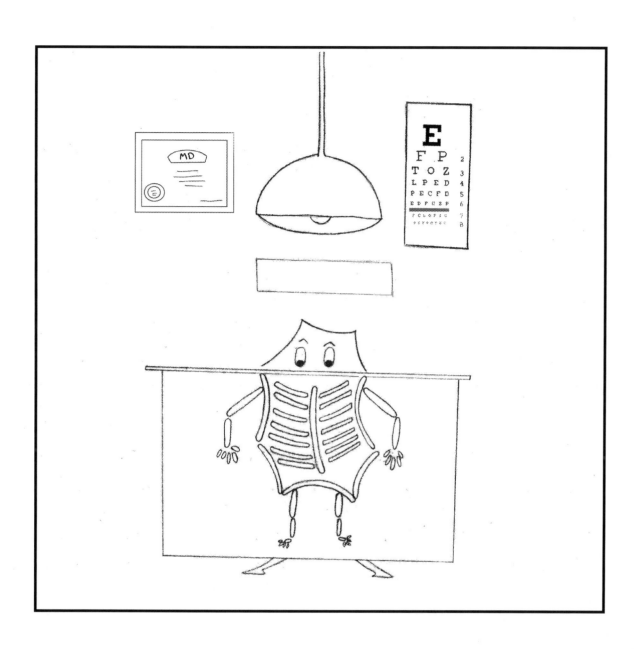

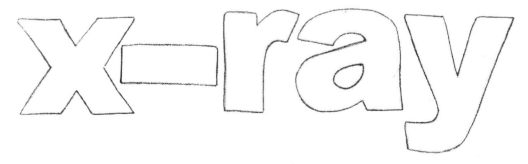

I went to the doctor to get an **X-ray**.

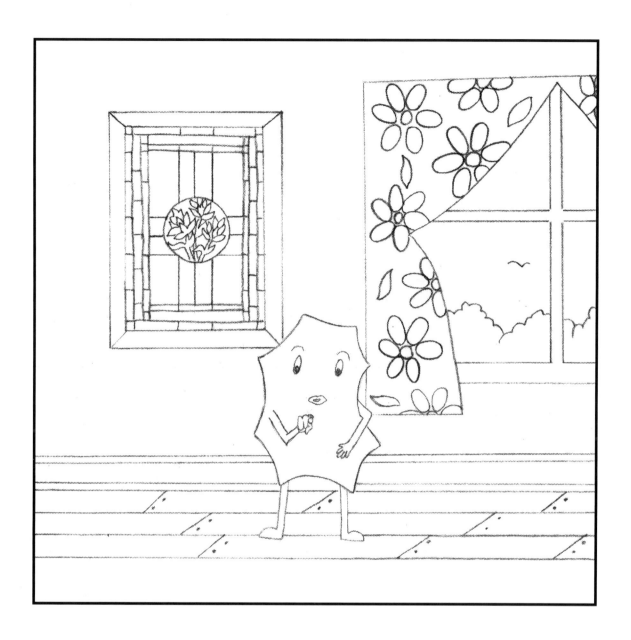

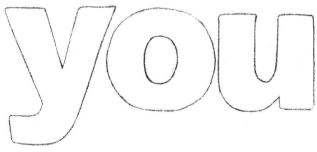

I like *you*.

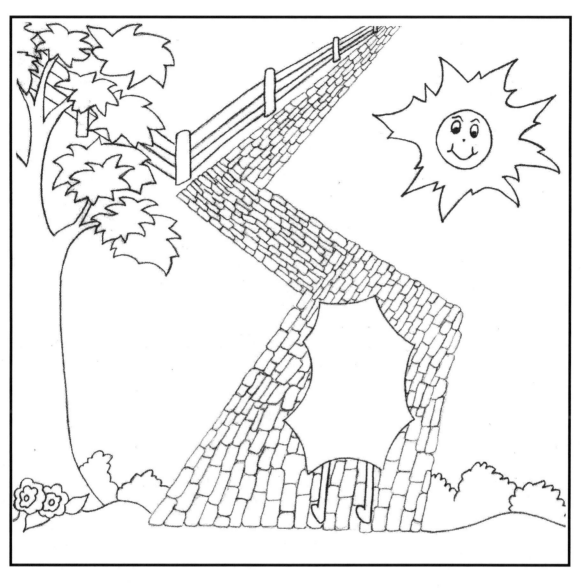

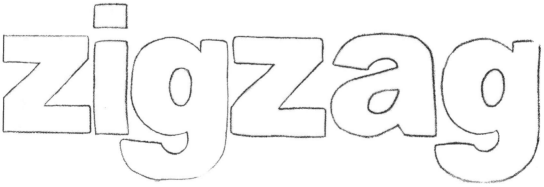

The road home goes in a **zigzag**.

Printed in the United States
By Bookmasters